Why People Move

by Kelly Gaffney

a Capstone company — publishers for children

Engage Literacy is published in the UK by Raintree.
Raintree is an imprint of Capstone Global Library Limited, a company incorporated in England and Wales having its registered office at 264 Banbury Road, Oxford, OX2 7DY – Registered company number: 6695582

www.raintree.co.uk

Text copyright © Kelly Gaffney 2021
Lead authors Jay Dale and Anne Giulieri

Editorial credits
Erika L. Shores, editor; Kayla Rossow, designer; Eric Gohl, media researcher; Laura Manthe, production specialist

Image credits
Alamy: Richard Levine, 23 (top); Getty Images: Culture Club, 9, Melanie Stetson Freeman, 19; iStockphoto: Juanmonino, 18, kali9, 13 (bottom), 20, Vesnaandjic, 1, 17 (bottom); Newscom: Glasshouse Images, 5, Sipa USA/Ronen Tivony, 21, Xinhua News Agency/Agung Kuncahya B., 10, ZUMA Press/Richard Lautens, 13 (top); North Wind Picture Archives: 7, 8; Shutterstock: Andriy Blokhin, 14, Attitude, background (throughout), carballo, back cover, 4, Everett Historical, cover (top), 11, Fabi Mingrino, 16, Mike Dotta, 23 (bottom), Monkey Business Images, cover (bottom), Rizd, 15, WIRACHAIPHOTO, 17 (top)

Why People Move

ISBN: 978-1-4747-9938-6

Printed and bound in the United Kingdom.

Contents

What does migrate mean?

People sometimes decide to live in a new place. They can move to a new town or city. They can even move to a new country. People move for lots of different reasons. Sometimes they want to move, but there are also times when people need to move.

People *migrate* when they go to live in a new place. People can move to a new place and stay there forever. Or they can move away but only stay for a few years. Large groups of people can decide to move to a new place together, but a person can also move by themselves.

5

When have people migrated?

People have always moved from place to place. Long ago, there were no towns or cities. There weren't any shops or even any farms. People had to find the food that they needed. They hunted animals and searched for plants that they could eat. This made it hard to stay in one place.

Sometimes people moved to a different place when the seasons changed. In the summer, they would move up into the mountains where it was cool. Then they would come down in the winter, when cold weather and snow made it hard to find food. These people had to migrate to survive, or stay alive.

A long time later, people around the world began building small farms. They grew plants that they could eat and kept animals for food. People also began to build houses and live in small towns. During these times, people still moved from place to place. They travelled to different towns to *swap* the things that they had for things that they needed. They also travelled a long way looking for new land where they could build their farms.

Over the last 400 years, large groups of people have moved from one part of the world to a different part. This has happened because people have been looking for better jobs, homes and other things to make their lives better. It has also happened because of *natural disasters*, such as *earthquakes* and *floods*. When too much rain falls, floods can wash away roads and homes.

As *transport* became faster and cheaper, it was easier for people to move around. In the past, people needed horses, *wagons* and *carriages* to travel. Now there are boats, trains, buses, cars and planes. This has made it a lot easier for people to travel a long way.

DID YOU KNOW?

In the past, large groups of people moved together because it was safer that way.

Why do people move?

People migrate for many reasons. Sometimes people want to move. They may not like the place where they live. They might think it is too busy in a big city or too quiet in a small town. A new place may have different weather, too. Some people like hot weather, while other people like cool weather.

People also move to new places to be with their family and friends. Sometimes one family moves to a new city or country. Once they are used to the new place, other members of their family may move to the same place to be with them.

Sometimes people move because they have to. Some children spend a lot of time travelling to and from school. There are also children who can't go to school because it is just too far away. Some families decide to move so that their children have a good school close by.

People might move to a new place because their homes are not safe. Big storms and fires can make a place unsafe. People might move away until it is safe again, or they might decide to stay in a new place forever.

People also move for work. If there aren't enough jobs in one place, a person might have to move to a new place to find a job. People who work for their country's *army* often move depending on where they are needed. Sometimes people have other jobs which might mean they have to move to find work. For example, a *scientist* who learns about animals that live in the sea might have to move close to the ocean.

What is it like to move to a new place?

Moving to a new place can be scary at first. It can also be exciting. There are many new things to try and people to meet. You can go to a new school and make new friends.

You can also see different things. You might see snow for the first time or waves crashing on the beach. You might even see new kinds of animals.

You can learn different *activities* in a new place, too. If you move to a town or city near the beach, you might be able to go swimming in the ocean. You could go sailing or even learn how to ride a surfboard.

A new city or country will have delicious new foods that you can try, too! If you move to a warm place you might be able to eat new kinds of fruits. You can go to a new school that's close to home and make new friends. You may live in a larger house in a nicer place. Your dad or mum may have a new job that could give your family a better life.

Moving to a new place can also be hard. People sometimes get homesick. This means that they really miss their old home. People often miss their family and friends. They might even miss their favourite foods.

People sometimes find it hard in their new home because everything seems different. For example, if you move to a new country, you might have to learn to speak a new *language*. Food, clothes or other things may have different names. *Rules* that you have to follow may also be different, and it can make things a bit confusing for a while.

DID YOU KNOW?

People drive on the left-hand side of the road in some countries and the right-hand side of the road in other countries.

Most people soon settle into their new homes. Families go out and look around their new neighbourhood or city. They visit shops and picnic in the park.

People who are new to a place can join in *celebrations*, such as *parades* or watching fireworks. They can meet new people by joining clubs. They also meet up with other people who came from where they used to live. All of these things can help them feel less lonely.

How can you help new people in your town?

There are things you can do to help new people in your town. If someone is new to your school, you can show them where things are. You can also make sure that they have someone to play with or sit with at lunch time. Try to understand if someone doesn't know the way things are done in your town or school. Help someone who is new to learn about rules or things that are done differently. Ask them to join in town and school activities. Take time to learn about things they like to do.

When people come into new towns, they bring ideas, interesting celebrations and delicious foods. Get to know the children who move to your school. You could make a friend and you might learn something new!

Glossary

activities things people do for fun

army a group of soldiers who work to protect a country

carriages vehicles with wheels that are usually pulled by horses

celebrations gatherings with activities on a special day

earthquakes strong shaking or trembling of the ground

floods water overflowing its normal limits

language the way people speak or talk

migrate to move from one place to another

natural disasters earthquakes, floods, storms or other deadly events caused by nature

parades lines of people, bands, cars and floats that travel along a street

rules instructions telling people what to do

scientist a person who studies the world around us

swap to trade or exchange one thing for another

transport a way to move from one place to another

wagons vehicles with wheels that move heavy loads

Index